3 5674 00949777 8

W9-BXF-649

DETROIT PUBLIC LIBRARY

CL

DATE DUE

3 1 MAR 2000

NOV 0 4 2000

NOV 2 4 2000

© Aladdin Books Ltd.

Designed and produced by
Aladdin Books Ltd.
70 Old Compton Street
London W1

First published in
the United States in 1984 by
Franklin Watts,
387 Park Avenue South,
New York, NY 10016

0-531-04771-7

Printed in Belgium

Contents

Masks and Puppets

Consultant Caroline Pitcher

Illustrated by Louise Nevett

Franklin Watts
London · New York · Toronto · Sydney
1984

About this book

J 602
M37
c.2

The projects in this book are designed for children to make by themselves or with a group of friends. Children can follow the sequence of instructions through pictures, whether or not they can read. The text is included for the parent/teacher to give additional hints and tips.

The "What you need" panel shows clearly what is required for each project. No supervision is required – except where this symbol appears ⚠.

The materials needed for the projects are usually available in most homes or classrooms. Where certain materials may not be available, alternatives are given. It is a good idea to collect all sorts of household bits and pieces. See Page 30.

The level of difficulty of the projects varies slightly to cater to children of differing abilities.

 Where this symbol appears, adult help is required. Look for it.

Cutting

Children should never be given sharp knives or scissors, and for most projects in this book they are unnecessary. There are many types of children's scissors available with rounded ends. Where objects are difficult to cut – for example, potatoes or plastic dish-washing liquid bottles – an adult should supervise. These instances are marked with the danger symbol. Where a plastic bottle is specified, be sure that it does not contain any dangerous liquids such as bleach or disinfectant. Always rinse out bottles, whatever they have contained.

Gluing

Any sort of paste or glue is suitable for making most of the projects, but in certain cases a strong glue is required and this is illustrated with a red asterisk on the glue pot. An adult should supervise when strong glue is being used.

Coloring

Most projects can be successfully colored with powder paint or ordinary watercolor. For shiny or plastic surfaces use poster paint, powder paint, or tempura paint mixed with a PVA medium. Look for the AP or CP seal of approval. Where projects are to be used in water, use wax crayons to color them.

Powder paint, poster paint, and wax crayons are all nontoxic and lead-free. Alternative coloring methods are colored pencils (crayons), or felt-tip pens and pastels. Ensure that the felt-tips you use are nontoxic.

One of the simplest ways of applying color is to cut out the required shape from colored paper and glue it onto the project.

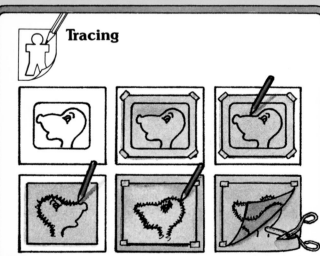

Tracing

Where a tracing outline appears it is labeled with the tracing symbol. Tape the tracing paper over the outline. Trace the outline. Turn over the tracing and rub a pencil thickly on the back. Tape the tracing, outline upward, on paper or cardboard, and retrace the outline.

JUL '86.

What you need:

What the symbols mean

Glue

Strong glue

Scissors

Paint

Kitchen knife

Pencil

Paintbrush

Fat felt-tip pen

Thin felt-tip pen

Wax crayon

Paper

Thin cardboard

Thick cardboard

Tracing paper

Tinfoil

Pipe cleaner

Rubber band

Toothpicks

Drinking straw

Modeling clay

String

Yogurt or cream container

Coin

Cork

Cotton thread spool

Popsicle stick

Bottle cap

Small cardboard roll

Matchbox lid

Matchbox tray

Used matchsticks

Scotch tape

Small box

Large cardboard roll

Dish-washing liquid bottle

Knitting yarn

Milk or juice carton

Large box

Humpty Plate Puppet

- Two paper plates are ideal, but you can make circles by drawing around a plate and cutting them out.
- Trace the nose and bow tie from picture 1.
- Use pipe cleaners, clay and corks for the arms and legs.

What you need:

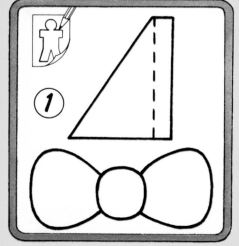

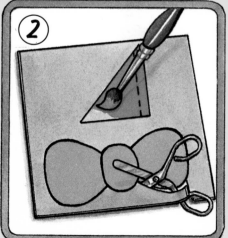

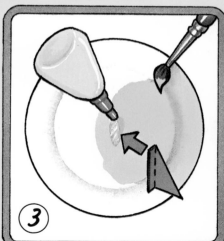

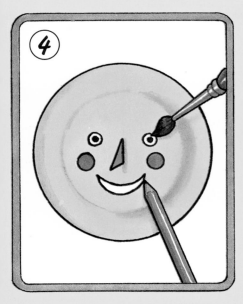

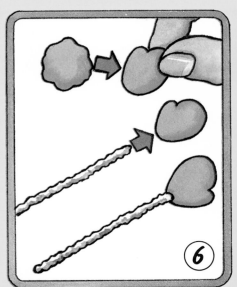

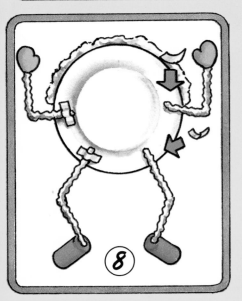

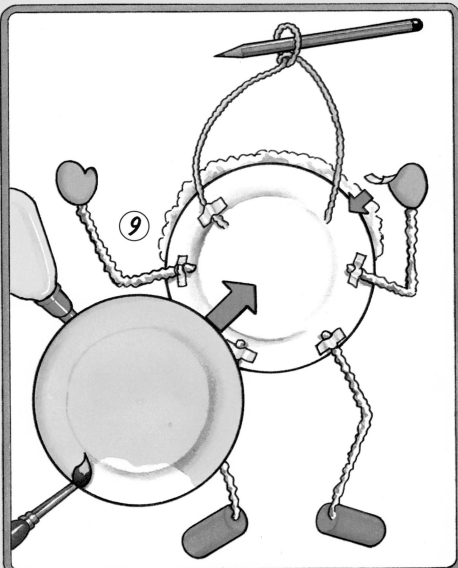

Clown Mask

What you need:

- ● Cut an oval shape from cardboard approximately the size of your face.

- ● Draw the clown's face on it using the simple design in picture 3 as a guide.

- ● Remember to make holes for the eyes.

- ● You can glue tufts of knitting yarn or cotton ball to the mask to make a different face.

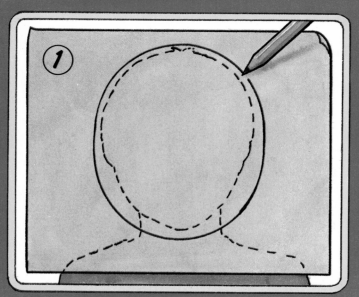

①

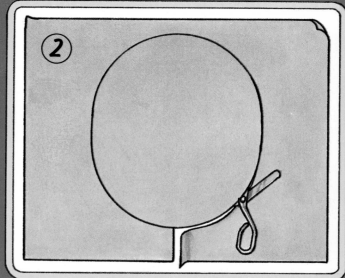

②

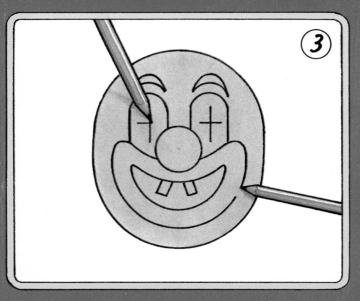

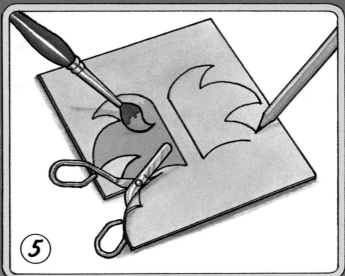

9

Sock Muppet

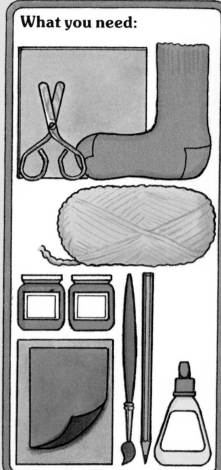

- Use any old sock or a thick stocking cut to size for this project.

- Be sure to make the cut – picture 1 – on the top of the foot of the sock.

- Trace the eyes from the outline in picture 5. Trace the mouth from the outline in picture 7.

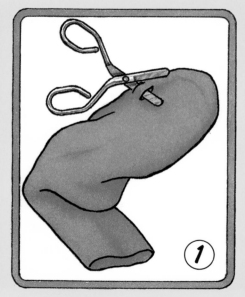

①

②

③

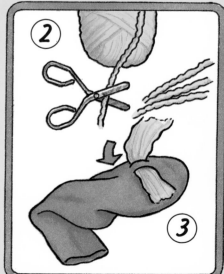

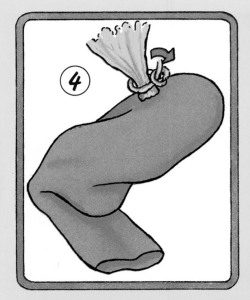

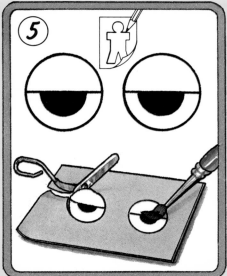

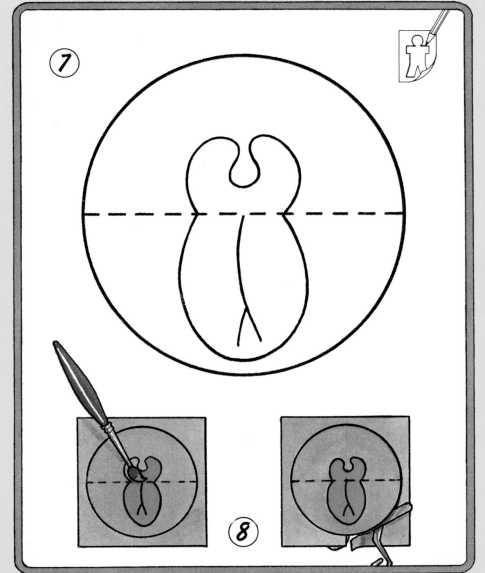

Knights' Helmet

- Cut a strip of cardboard high enough to cover the area from your shoulders to above your head.

- Measure it around your head for a comfortable fit and glue it together.

- Attach the visor to the helmet with pieces of pipe cleaner or knot of string.

What you need:

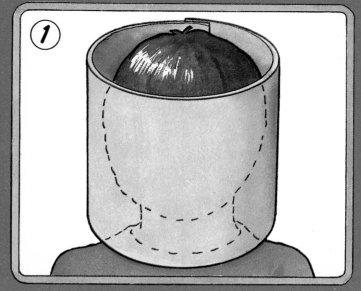

1

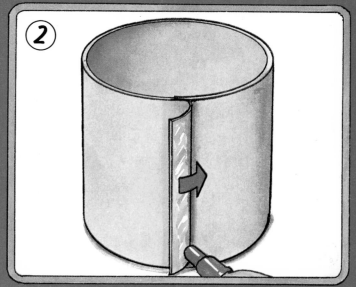

2

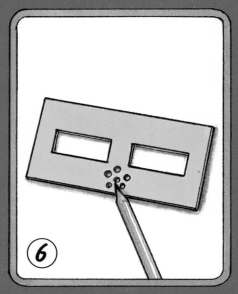

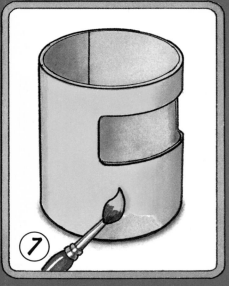

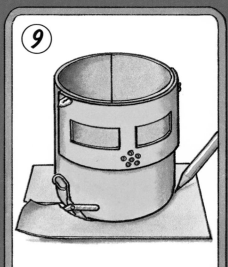

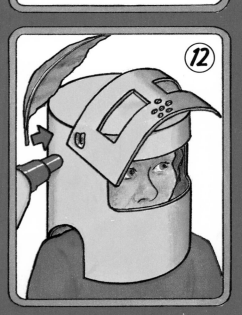

Pipe Cleaner Puppet

- Use any old sock or a thick stocking cut to size for this project.
- Put tufts of knitting yarn or string into the hole in the toe and secure it with string or thread.
- Tape a ball of newspaper and stick it into the toe. Fasten with string or thread.
- Make the arms from left-over sock and attach pipe cleaners to them so you can move them as you like.

What you need:

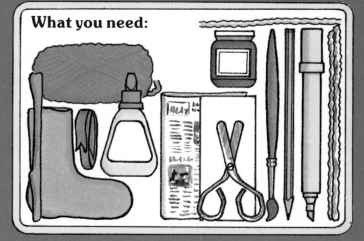

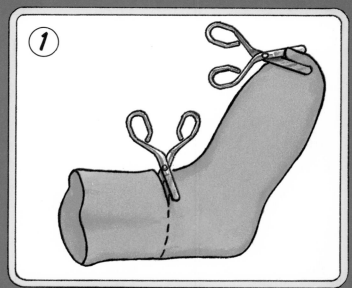

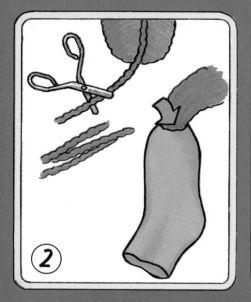

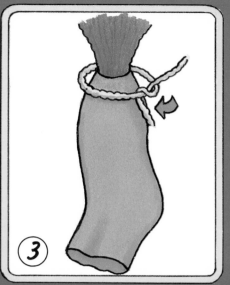

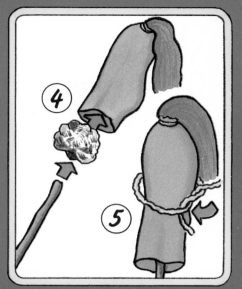

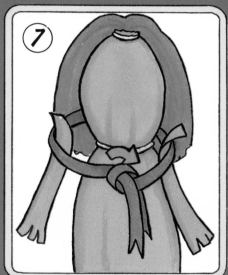

Tiger Mask

● Draw around a plate to make the circle. Remember to draw the ears, using a cup, before cutting it out.

● Copy the tiger design shown – or make up your own. The circle of cardboard on a stick is all you need to start.

What you need:

①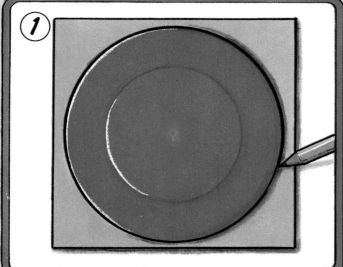

②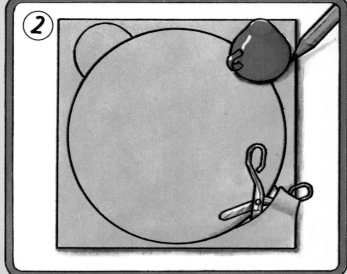

16

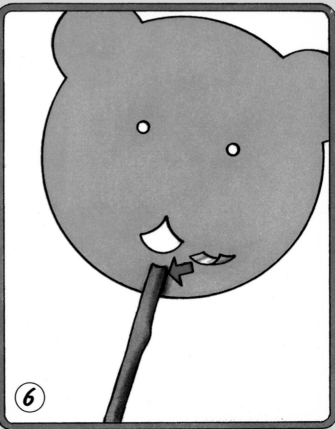

Mouse Finger Puppet

- Twist a narrow strip of paper around your finger to make a cone and glue together.

- Put the puppet on your middle finger, and your thumb and other fingers become its legs.

What you need:

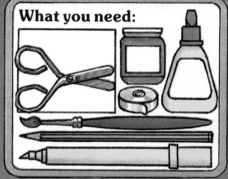

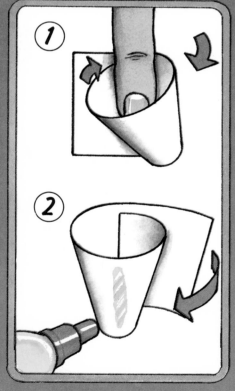

① ②

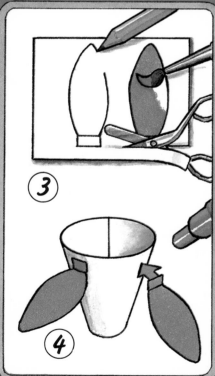

③ ④

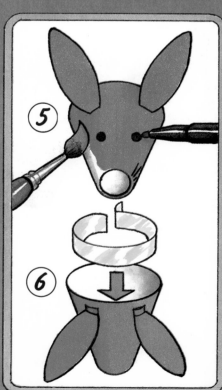

⑤ ⑥

Dancing Finger Puppet

- Copy the designs onto cardboard as shown.
- Make them dance by putting two fingers through the holes.
- You can also make up your own designs for dancing puppets.

What you need:

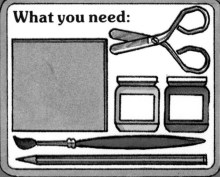

①

②

③

Jack-o'-lantern

- Children may need help in cutting the pumpkin. Do not give them a sharp knife.
- Fasten on a knotted string for carrying it.

What you need:

①

②

Stick Clown

- Mix flour and water to make the paste into which strips of newspaper are dipped.

- Make sure that the papier mâché is completely dry before bursting the balloon inside it.

- You may need to secure the head to the stick with plasticine or glue.

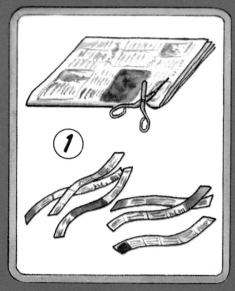

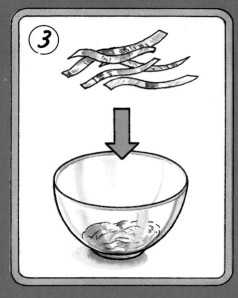

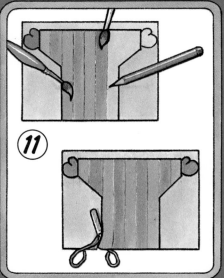

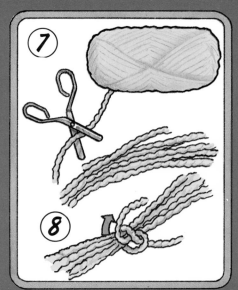

Walking Bird

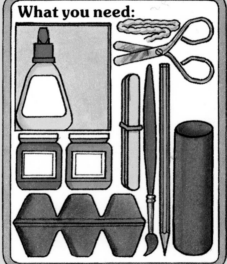

- A cardboard tube is best for the bird's body. Or you can roll a sheet of cardboard and stick it together.

- Take care when cutting the lengths of yarn so that the bird will balance when complete.

What you need:

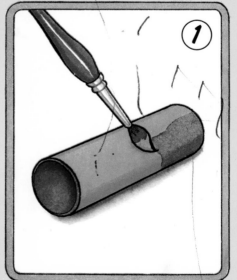

(1)

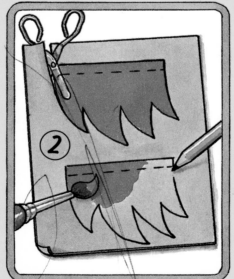

(2)

(3)

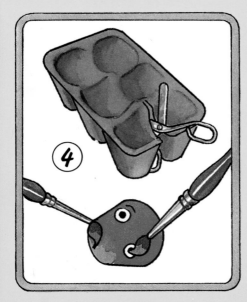

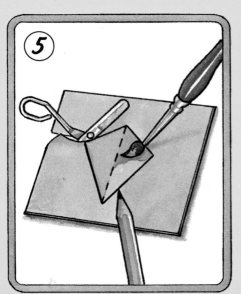

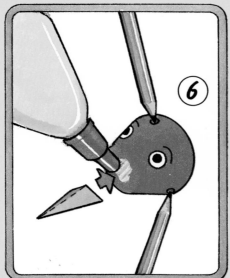

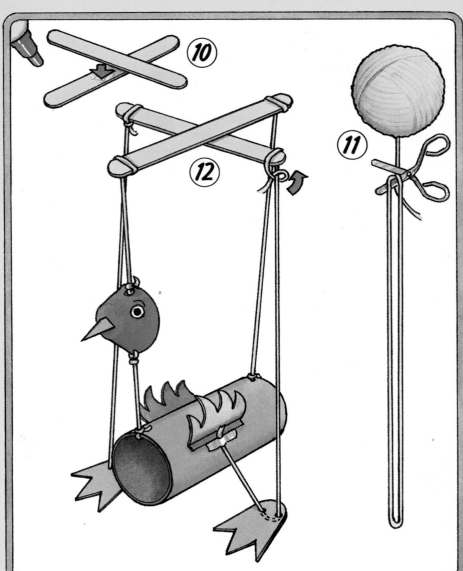

"Keystone Kop"

- Trace the shapes to make the "kop" from pictures 1, 2, 3 and 4.

- From picture 4 you need two shoes, four parts for upper arms and upper legs, and four parts for lower arms and lower legs.

What you need:

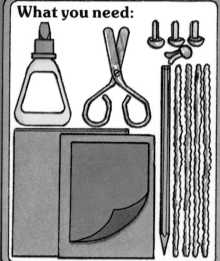

①

②

③

26

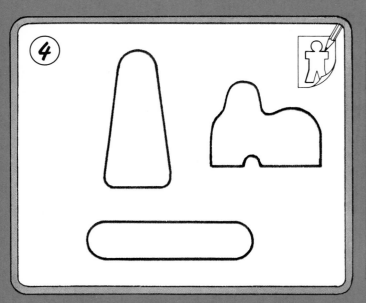

Puppet Theater

- You need a very large carton to make this project.

- When complete, balance the theater on the backs of two chairs. Hang a cloth over the chairs and you can sit behind the cloth and give your own puppet show.

What you need:

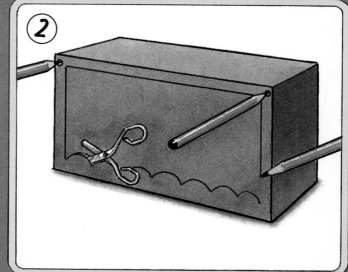

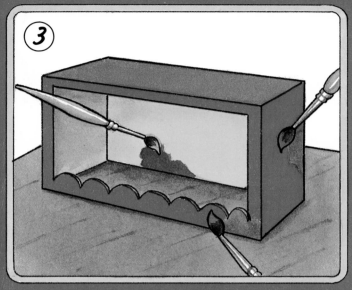

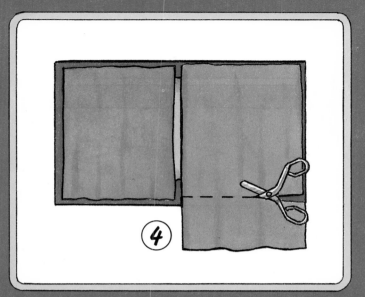

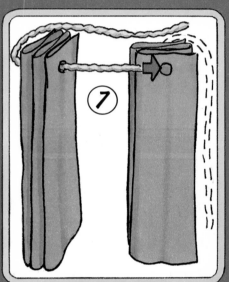

Bits Box

Collect all sorts of household bits and pieces on a regular basis. Children can use them not only for making the projects in this book, but also for inventing models of their own. Here are a few suggestions, but anything at all may prove useful with a bit of imagination. Keep everything together in a "bits box."

Projects conceived by Aladdin
Art Editor Malcolm Smythe

PRINTED IN BELGIUM BY

INTERNATIONAL BOOK PRODUCTION